Coloring Books For BOYS

Cool Cars And Vehicles

I0443216

this notebook belongs to :

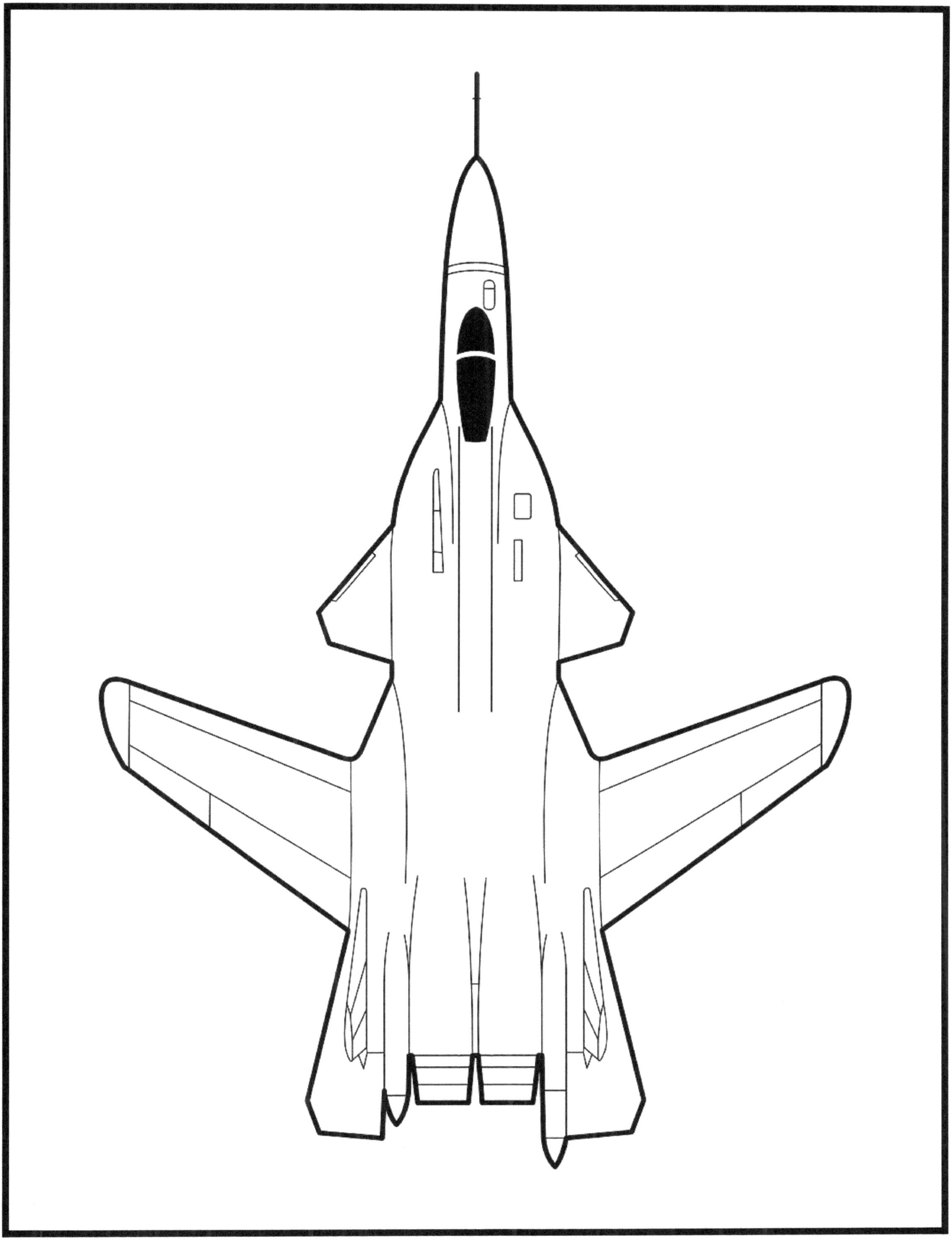

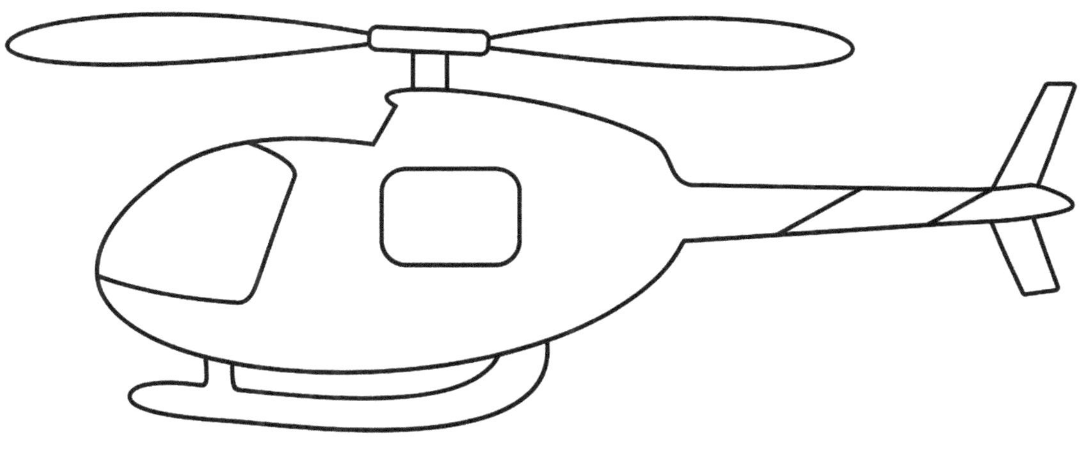

SS
SS

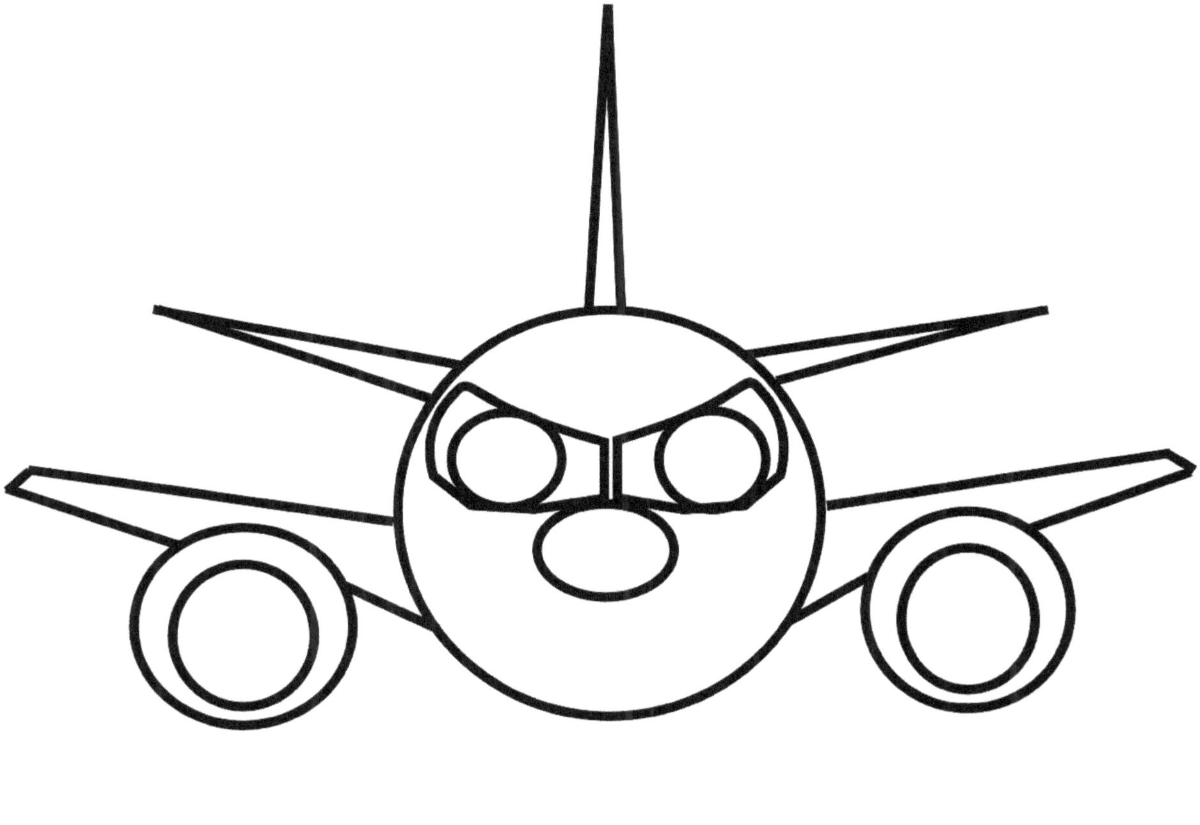

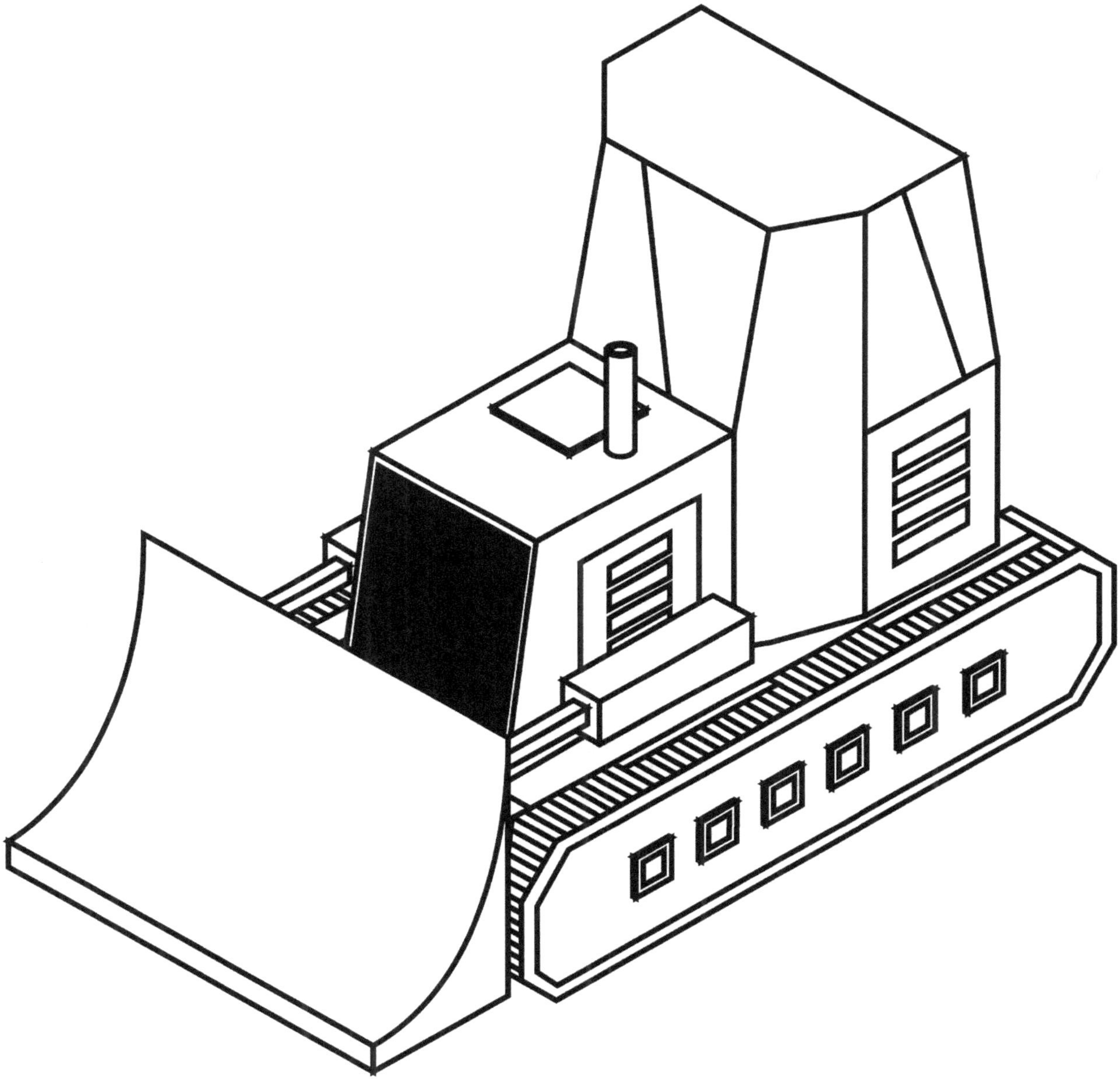

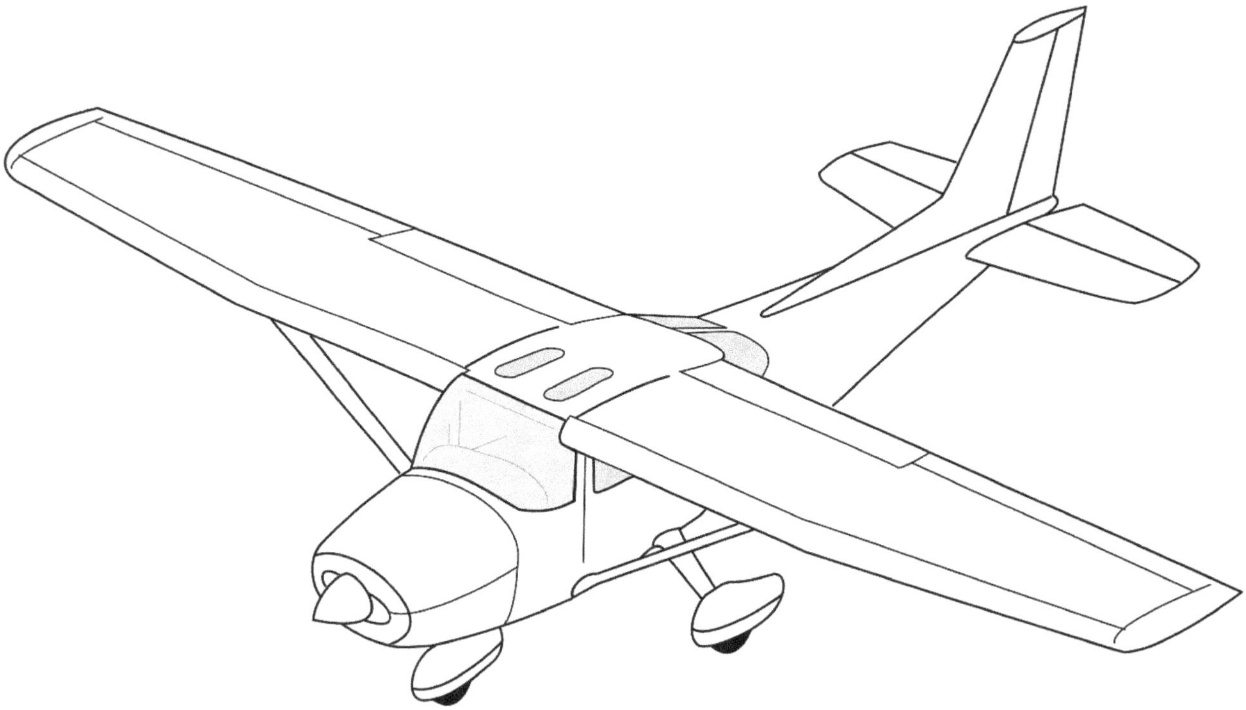

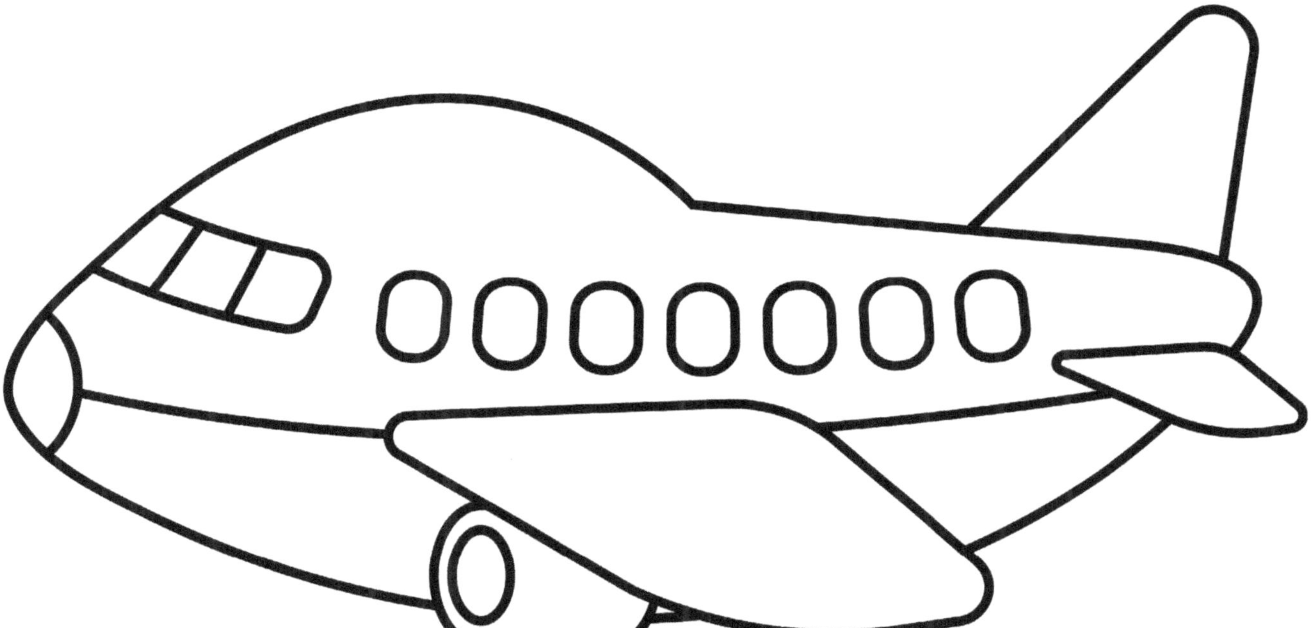

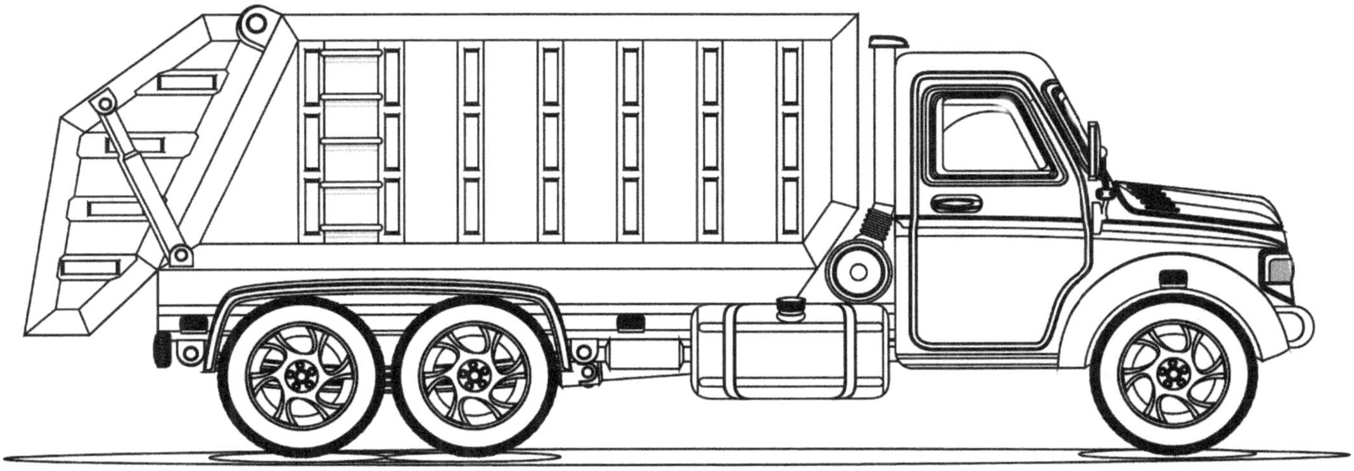

NYC TAXI

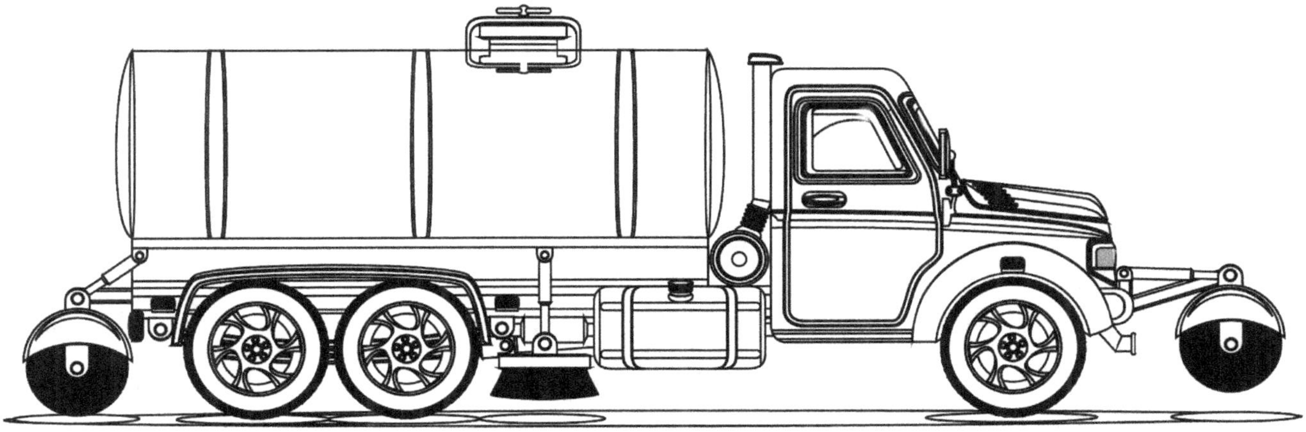

NYC TAXI

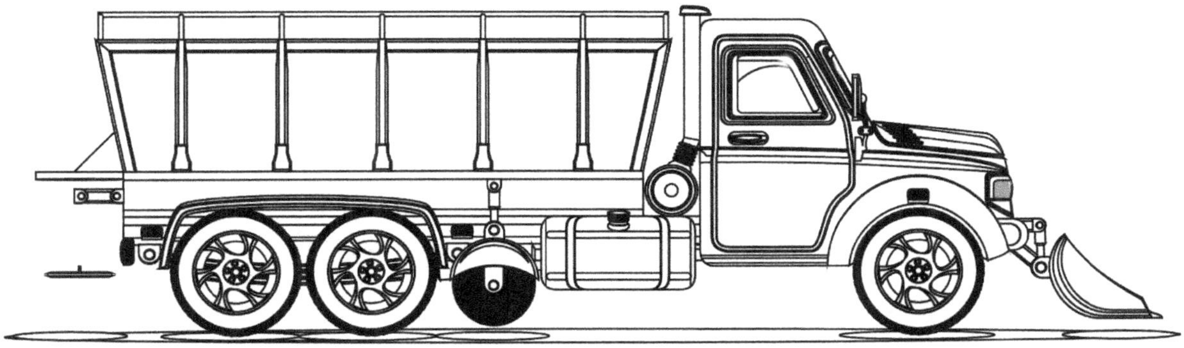

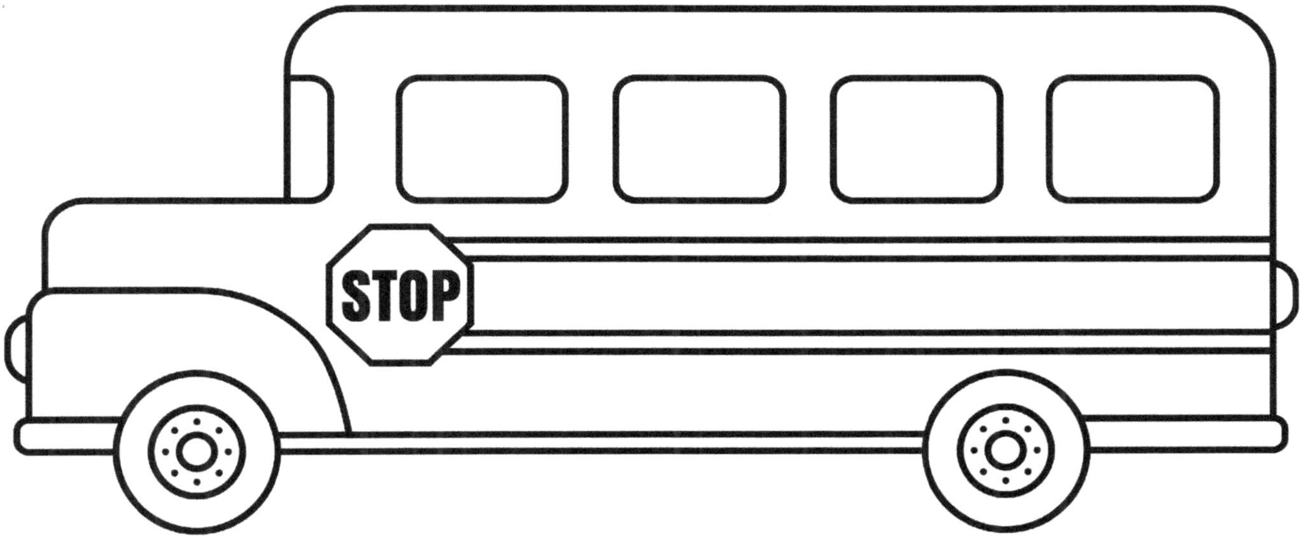
STOP

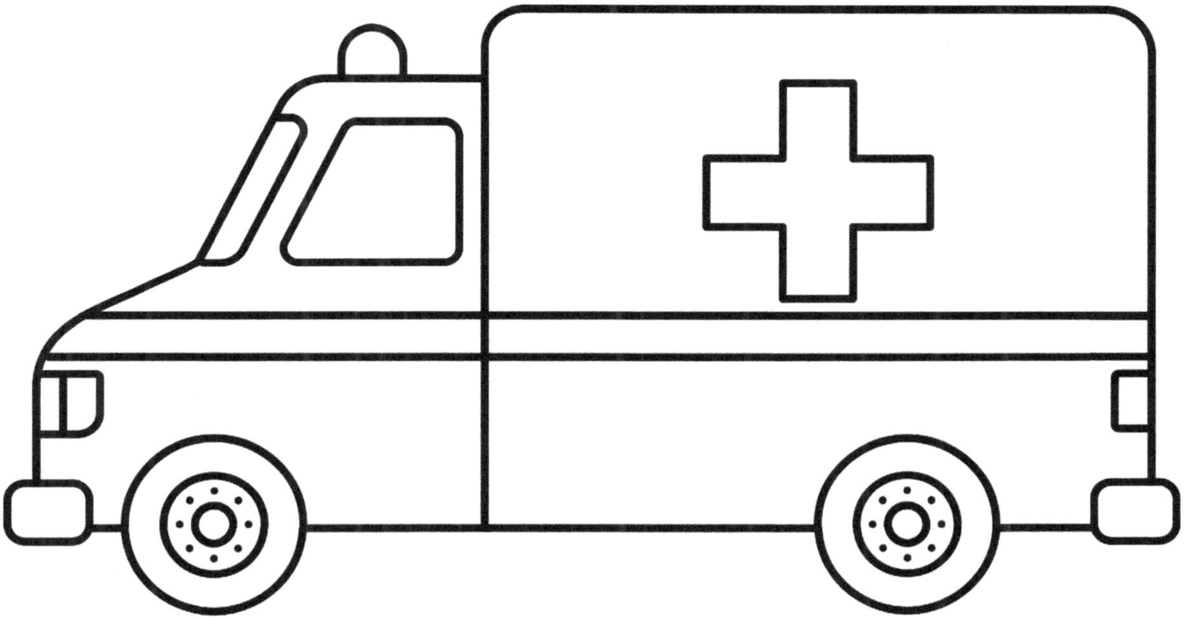

Fresh Bread

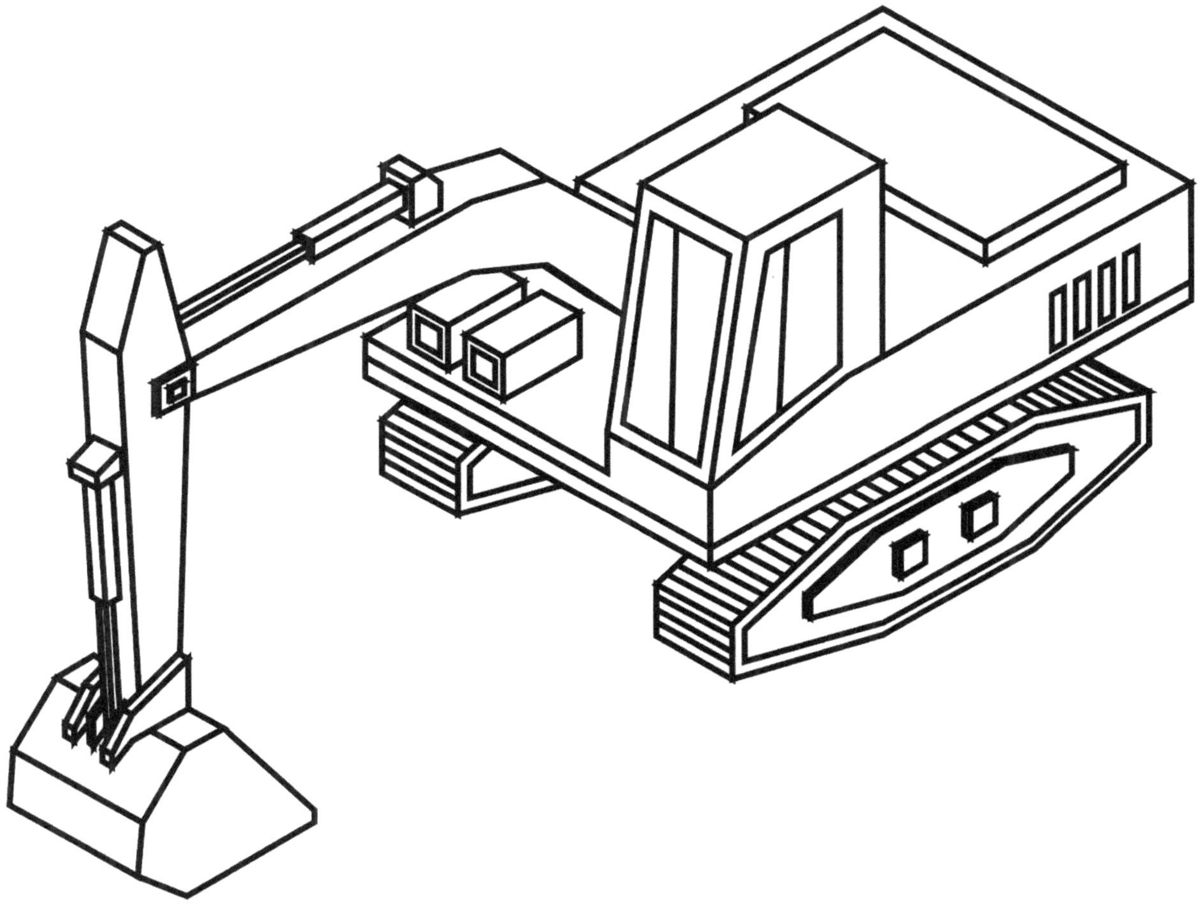

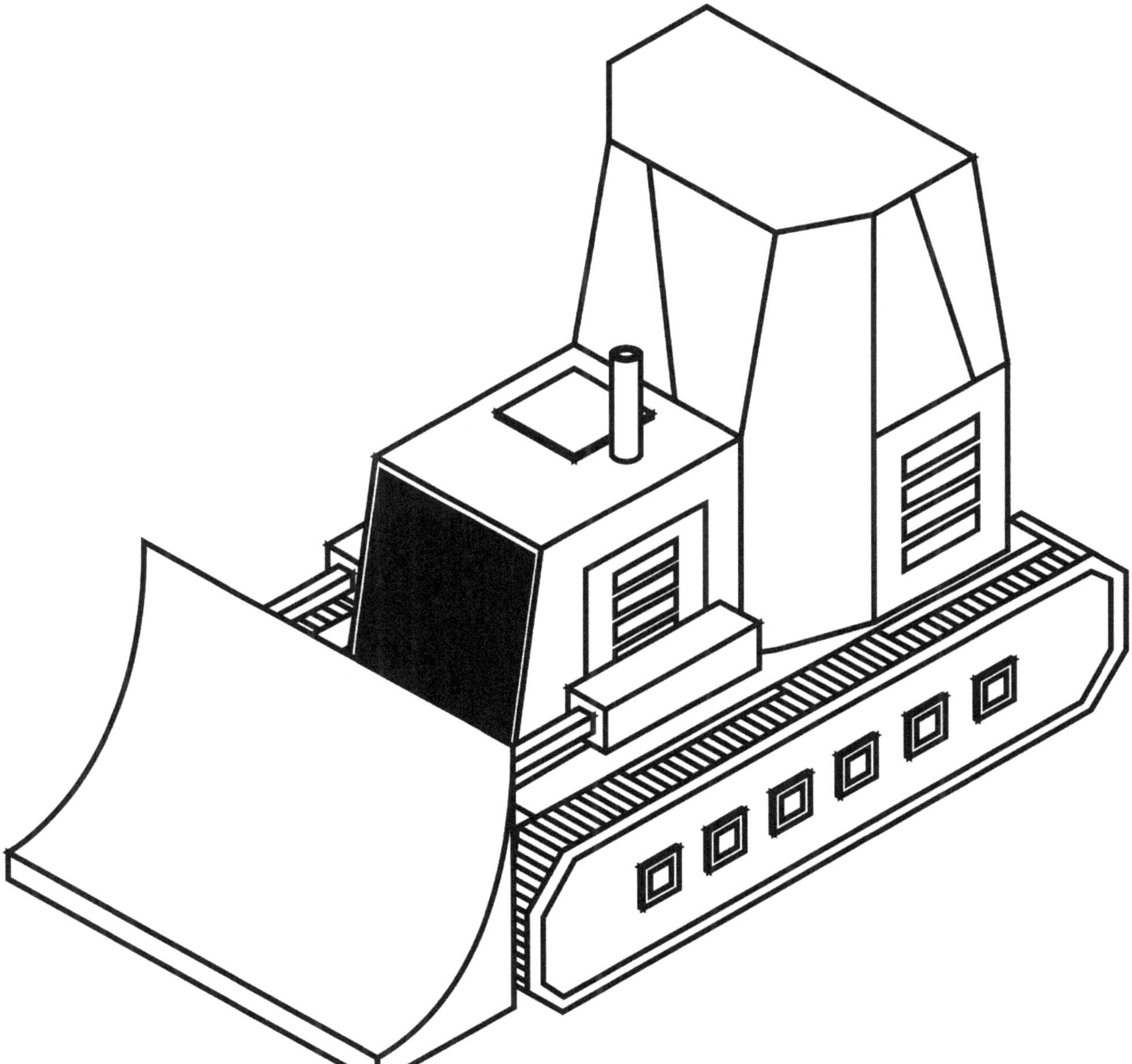

www.ingramcontent.com/pod-product-compliance
Lightning Source LLC
Chambersburg PA
CBHW080603220526
45466CB00010B/3240
* 9 7 9 8 5 8 9 5 4 5 6 7 8 *